All The Things I Never Said

All The Things I Never Said

All pieces written by Mae Krell
Cover art drawn by Tiffany Tremaine

For you;
and no there is not
only one
"you"
There are many you's.
and those you's
know who they are.

They know how I spent countless hours
thinking about them
and even more
writing about them.
and this is all the words
I didn't say to them.

So to you,
if you are reading this
please understand why
I did not open my mouth
to speak
when I should have
and I hope
all of
these
explain what I would have said.

Introduction:

Writing is hard, you know. The fact that you're just supposed to sit down and have a million thoughts flow into your head is crazy. You could have a week where nothing but sadness floods your mind and you can't think of anything and then you can have one day where your mind decides to change and goes wild with happy thoughts of even the stupidest things. So if you ask me how I think of what to write, I mean, I have no idea. They come to me, and sometimes they suck, but that doesn't mean I don't write them down.

You need to write everything. The good and the bad and the sad and the happy, because one day you'll look to the past and decide to read what you had written a while back. and I guess when you do you'll be reminded of the friends, the breakups, the love, the loss, the ups, the downs, the rain and the sun. and I guess by then you'll realize that's all part of life. and life can be shitty. but fuck it. just live. One morning, any morning, you need to wake up and say to yourself, what the hell have you been doing until now, and you need to go out and live, because frankly, that's all life's got to offer.

So this is me. Living. A 14 year old girl publishing a book of the only feelings she's ever known how to express, in the only way she knows how to express them. So I tried. I tried and I tried and I tried to express my feelings the "right" way. In the way of words you can hear, in speech. But that's never worked out for me much. It seems a little weird to me, to speak, if no one is listening. So for a while, when I was younger, I used to talk a lot. And I would babble on and on, and one day, I realized that, frankly, no one cared.

no one was listening

no one cared.

So, I went on to express my feelings the way I knew how to. And speaking was not that way. At the time writing wasn't either. And my way of expressing my feelings, wasn't very helpful to anyone, especially not to me, even though I thought it was. Then last year, I discovered the glorious form of self expression and therapy that is writing. And I have not put the pen down since. Whenever I have something to say, I write it down, instead of well, saying it. And this is a collection of that. A collection of the happy words, the crying words, the bleeding words, and most of all the words I couldn't physically move my vocal chords to get out of my mouth. Sometimes its hard, saying what you feel, advocating for who, or what you love. And that's ok, because no matter how easy everyone makes it seem, or no matter how easy everyone says it is, It's not easy. It's not easy for anyone, it just comes more naturally to some, then it does to others. And that doesn't mean one of us, is unequal, or inadequate, it just means one of us has to work a little harder to achieve greatness, and there is absolutely nothing wrong with that.

I am trying, no. I am going. With this book, with my writing, with me, whoever that is, to seek a great perhaps, because that's what we all try to do, and that's what we all want. So I guess, yeah, this is a collection of my words. All bunched together into this book you are holding or the file you are reading it on. But that doesn't make it any less important. You. go, and pick up the pen, and just write.
and write. and write.
everything you've always wanted to say and couldn't.
and when you're done with your writing, go on to read mine. Go on to read the words that all together make up all the things I never said.

The Seasons Of People

Summer;
i fell for a boy
who loved the beach
because he said that in the waves
he could hear
all the voices of those
who had been silenced
by the creatures
who walked the sand

Fall;
I fell for a boy
who always asked me
how i was doing
and cared for me
more than he did
for himself
but really, he needed more caring
than i did

Winter;
I fell for a boy
who seemed to love himself
more than he loved
anyone else
but really
he felt like he was the worst
so he acted as if
he was the best

Spring;
I fell for a boy
who loved the rain
every time
he saw the sky's tears
he would run out
and stand in the middle of the street
so i would chase him
and then complain

because the rain was messing up my hair
or my outfit
and he would always say
"That's because
you aren't feeling the rain
all you're doing
is getting wet"

When spring left
he left too
and i wept
like the sky did
hoping he would come back
to feel the rain
again

Beauty

Did you ever wonder why
in animals
hip bones
collar bones
and
rib cages
being visible
are thought of as
sickly
ugly
and sometimes even abusive
yet, in humans
that is what we call
                    beautiful

Hopes And Dreams
(For Allison)

There are many things i hope for in life
i hope that one day
you will go and buy every dress
you've ever wanted
i hope that one day
you'll dance barefoot in wet grass and laugh
i hope that one day
you start to notice everything beautiful around you
like flowers
and small kittens
i hope that one day
you'll go visit every small city and large country you want to
and travel to your heart's content
i hope that one day
you'll stop worrying about all those things
that are out of your control
and one day i hope you decide
to speak up for what you believe in
and step out of your comfort zone
i hope that one day
you'll fall in love
with that one boy
who you love even more
than you love yourself
and lastly
i hope that one day
you'll forget all the pain you've endured
and just learn
to be happy

Those Nights

And every night
I am haunted by the fact
that
all these memories
that mean the world to me
you probably
don't even remember
and how
now
I don't matter to you
at all

Definitions

What is time?
Is it the ticking clock
hanging on the wall
or is it
the way the sun rises and sets
on the horizon in summer
is it the way a child grows
over the course of seasons
or is it the hourglass on my table
counting the seconds
until who knows when
So when you said you wanted me to
"give you time"
i brought you the clock from my wall
and i took you to watch the sun
rise and set
i showed you photos
of a child growing
and i brought you my hourglass
instead of leaving it on my table
to count the seconds
until forever

so now
when you say to "give you time"
what am i supposed to do?
because i would cross oceans
to bring you what you want
i will do anything for you
except leave your side

So when you told me
you needed to be alone
i told you that was the one thing
i could not do
because without you
my clock stops ticking
and my seasons stop changing
and the hourglass sitting

on my table
stops counting seconds
because for me,
without you
there is no forever

Human Invisibility

You said
you didn't care
for me
anymore
so you went
your way
and i went
your way too
but when you looked
my way
you saw nothing
because to you
i had become
invisible.

The End

Goodbye
is the hardest word to say
because goodbye
means leaving
and leaving
means drifting
and drifting
means forgetting

but no matter how far away
i am from you
you will always
be with me
because well
you've made your impact
on me
in a way
no one else
could have

so,
well thank you
and goodbye
and hopefully
you won't forget
the color of my eyes
or my smile
and hopefully
my memory
will linger in your mind
like the stars do
when the dark rises
but not drift away
when night creeps out

because well
when you forget the color of my eyes
i will soon forget yours too
and then your memory

will drift away
and eventually
all i'll have left
is the taste
of coffee tainted kisses
and the lingering memory
of you

The Happiest Of Sads

How could you make
my lips
curve upwards in happiness
and
my eyes close and open
while dropping waves of tears
onto the shore
that is my face
at the same time?

Jumbeled Thoughts

Half of the time
I don't know what i'm writing about
half of the time
words spill out of me
like a cluster of nothing
half of the time
i think about the rain and the sun
and about how
time has lots of parts
and halves
but really
half of the time
my words
my thoughts
and my feelings
just think
of you

Shoot

What is more powerful
a thought, or a gun?

a gun gives the opportunity
but a thought
pulls the trigger

A Wilting Lie

You gave me flowers
and told me that
as long as they live
our love
will too

But those flowers
are slowly wilting
and you are not
by my side.

Just because
these flowers are damaged
and broken
does not mean
they are not alive

These flowers are still alive
and our love should be too
but it is not
and you are not
here
by my side

so I guess
you lied

Breakdowns

Her mind was flooded with thoughts of him
but unfortunately
she couldn't swim

Untitled 1 (about you)

You are the kind of mystery
that I would love to spend
the rest of my life
trying to unravel

3 in the morning

You don't really know someone
until you've talked to them
at 3
in the morning

3 in the morning
is when words
are most sincere
and eyelids
are slowly sinking.
the hour
when the most genuine thoughts
and opinions
come out

But when you
are alone at
3 in the morning
everything you have ever tried to forget
comes flooding back at once
like a tsunami tide
and all your demons collide
and all you can hope for
is that if you close your eyes
it'll all go away

But when it doesn't
what do you do then?
some people choose to overdose
some to drink
or to smoke
and some take pills
because it would be nice
to sleep for a while
a coma maybe
or a long nap
anything to escape.
anything to get rid of these thoughts
these feelings

Late Nights

It's 4:14 am
and my mind
has been completely corrupted
and flooded
with thoughts
of you

Every Bird Has A Broken Song

If you're a bird
i'm a bird
but if you expect me to stay with you
after you push me
off our little tree
or after you treat me badly
and hurt me
I won't

Maybe the first time
i'll stay
and maybe the second time
i will too

But soon later
when you push me down
I won't be able to get up
and maybe my wing
will be hurt
and I won't be able
to fly anymore

And then what will you do?
will you help me,
or will you continue sitting
in what used to be
our
little tree
and watch me fall?

Blinded

I loved you
but you didn't love me

and sure
that was sad
but really
the worst thing was
that even though you knew
I loved you
you acted like
no one did

Because your everything
was this person who didn't
care about you
just like my everything
is you
and you don't care
about me

Childhood Sayings

They always say
"you are what you eat"
and then they wonder
why I don't eat
at all

Four Twenty Two

At 4:21 am
I sit in my room
and think
about what it would be like
to still be with you
At 4:21 am
I sit in my room
and i think about
what it would be like
to be happy again

At 4:21 am
I sit in my room
and I wonder what it's like
for your new girlfriend
who wakes up every morning
to that sweet sleepy voice of yours

And I wonder what it's like
being your favorite mug
that she always pours
your coffee into
the one
that gets to kiss your lips
every morning

And really
it's not you
that I miss
even though it seems
that way sometimes

no
it's not you I miss
it's the memories we had
and the fact that
you actually cared
about me
and that I had someone to talk to

at 4:21 am

And now it's
4:22 am
and I have
finally realized
that I am
alone

Empty Heart

When you were with me
you mended my broken heart
by sewing in small parts of you

but when you left
I felt empty
because all of those parts of me
didn't have you in them
anymore

Hidden Insanity

What is real insanity?
and who is really insane?
I asked him.

He hesitated,
then opened his mouth to speak
"the ones who are truly insane
are the people who believe
they are not.
the ones who believe
that they
are aways ok"

but truth is,
we all go mad sometimes
and that small break into
insanity
is actually
what keeps us
sane.

For Katelyn and Tiffany

You're beautiful
the words
that slowly seep out
of your light pale pink lips
and your green eyes
which are places perfectly
on your flawless face

so why is it
that with all of this
i'm still caught staring
straight
at your wrist
at those
rigid cuts
and small
bruises running up it

I wonder what happened
I wonder what your story is
I wonder;
if you knew
how beautiful
and talented
and well,
amazing
you really are
I wonder if you knew,
would you still be
doing this to yourself?

Gone

She had only meant
to go to sleep
but the sea;
it rocked her
and in it's waves
she drowned
in a sadness
so sweet
it engulfed her
(4:22 am)

Words

If your words
cut as deep
as my blade
I would be dead by now
and all of this
would be less painful

Not Everything Can Be Hidden

Some nice accessories
makeup
and a new outfit
won't hide how abused i've been

And a large house
glass doors
and a nice little garden
can't hide how broken this family is

Just because something has
a nice
expensive
new looking exterior
doesn't mean the interior
isn't broken
and bent

Not everything can be hidden
behind a pair of nice glass doors,
you know.
after all

The doors are transparent
and so are the people
trying to hide behind them

Summer

She was all alone
empty even
and no one knew
if she was ever there
or not

And oh
they called her summer
because she was really
only appreciated
when she was gone

Death In the Stars

I kinda believe people die when their fire burns out, you know, that fire that kinda keeps you going. Stars too, all they are, are balls of fire and they take years and years and years to burn out. I think when someone dies, they turn into a star and they get a fire that hardly ever burns out, unlike the ones they had as humans.

And stars, if you look up at night you can see, they light up the sky.. Technically if you figure out the science and do the math, if there was only one star, it could light up approximately the living space of one person by itself. I guess I think every person is assigned a star that shines on them and tries to help them keep their fire burning for as long they can before that person is ready to join them up there, as their own star.

Untitled 2
(About you)

For some reason
my mind cannot
find anything
that is worth
writing about

it's like
suddenly
this beautiful
colorful world
has become
black
and white

good and bad

sad and happy

with no
in between
but then
my brain wanders
and digs deep
into my thoughts

and what is left inside
are only images
of your beautiful
blue eyes
which I had once
gotten lost in
and your gorgeous brown hair
that matched perfectly
with your old combat boots
which you wore
no matter where
we went
and my mind is suddenly

completely occupied
and composed
of simple
thoughts
   of

you.

My sea

I am drowning
In my own sea of sadness
and I could save myself
If I just stood up

Floating (For Tiffany)

My knees are weak
but my soul is determined
and although I can't walk
my heart can fly
and sit itself right down
next to yours

and our hearts
can live happily together
until our minds
can meet

Dead Heart

Even though
my heart
is dead
it still
finds a way
to beat
for you

Days

There are good days, and bad days. Today was not a good day, but honestly, today was not a bad day either. Today was a day. Simply a day, nothing more and nothing less. Maybe tomorrow will be a good day, or maybe it will be a bad day, who knows, and frankly, who cares? Today is today, so why would I spend my time worrying about tomorrow. If anything, I should worry about today. I can worry about tomorrow when it comes.

Today is not a good day. And today is not a bad day. Today is a day. And I am completely okay with that.

Untitled 3

I feel bad
for those
who never
go crazy

Blurred Numbers

I counted the nights
since you left me

and on night number 12
I didn't know what to do
everything was so surreal
and it hit me
you are not
with me
anymore

and on night number 14;
I laid in my bed
cold
and alone
missing the sweet scent
of your cigarette stained lips
and the magnificent taste
of your coffee tainted kisses

and yet another night
I laid alone
wondering what it would feel like
to have you lye next to me again

and on night number 22
I finally realized
that it wasn't our adventures,
the words you said to me
or the way your eyes lit up
when you spoke of me
that I missed

It was you
and all the little things
that made that up
and I finally realized
that I could never feel this
for anyone else

because I am obsessively
and hopelessly
in love with you

and on the last night
night number 44
I saw a shooting star
and I wished
that you would come back

and I waited
and I waited

and I waited

but you never came
and that's kind of sad
if you think about it.

543
(For Tiffany)

We may be
543 miles away
but I feel connected to you
in everything I do
and everywhere I go
and I know
one day
you will be
here with me

Okay
(for Jill)

and I know
I swore to you
i'd be ok
but sometimes ok
isn't as happy
as it seems

sometimes ok is broken promises
and wasted nights
lying on the floor waiting
for someone to find you

sometimes ok
is hoping he wont leave
when you tell him
you've done it again
and you're so very sorry

sometimes ok
is hoping
that one day
you'll be "normal"
that maybe one day
you saying that you're ok
will actually mean
that you're fine

Suicidal and Cancerous

All the suicidal kids
with all their cuts and pills
no matter how hard they try
they just can't get it right
because they were born to live

All the cancerous kids
with all their smiles and tears
no matter how hard they try
they just can't get it right
because they were born
to die

{543 miles is bullshit, you're always in my heart}

Everything is nothing
until you have
someone to show it to
and share it with

Promises, Promises, But this time, It's different

and yes
I promise you tomorrow the sun will rise
and yes
I promise you tomorrow someone
will make you smile
and of course
when i'll walk the city streets
I'll think of you
and how I wish you were here

and shit
543 miles is pretty far
but eventually
you'll be here with me

and yes
I will walk
until my feet are nothing but blisters,
cuts and bruises
if that means
at the end of my journey
you'll be by my side
to heal my wounds
and tell me
It'll all
be ok

The Future

And I swear,
one day,
i'll be someone that I am not
and it'll be even greater
than who I am,
whoever that is.

Untitled 4
(About you)

And at the moment I first spoke to her, I already knew I would soon spend countless hours attempting to write a poem as beautiful as she is

Discoveries

Once you allow someone
to get close to you
they find a way
to get under your skin
and into the joints
that hold your fragile bones together

They add their own pieces
into your puzzle
until they feel that
they understand you

Once someone gets to this level
they are capable of writing full novels
simply based on the sound of your voice
when you have just woken up
or the way your lips taste
after your morning coffee

But they they decide
to reposition their pieces
in a different corner of your puzzle
and when they look around
they realize there is actually another
whole world
inside you
they they hadn't even
discovered yet

3 In The Morning

3ams
make me realize all the shit
we go through
to be happy

and it intrigues me
that there are actually people
who are able
to jump out of bed every morning
all happy and smiling
ready to face their day

most of the time
I go to war with my mind
over if I should get up
or not

and it kills me
It starts from the inside
and consumes me
slowly
and eventually
I cannot find a way
to breathe

Poisoned

You were addicted to her
like alcohol
every single day
you drank her up.
She was in
your veins
flowed through like blood.
Then you decided
to go sober.

Untitled 5
(About you)

I want to see
what your eyes look like
right before you start to cry
and I want to see
the way your pupils dilate
when you stay up way too late

I want to watch
the way your hair grows
and I want to know
what you smell like
and what it feels like
to have my arms
wrapped around you

I want to see you
and I want to get to know you;
for real this time

I want to spend my life
mapping out every single island
and river
on the globe
that is you
and I want to be the one
who hugs you tight enough
to mend all your broken pieces
back together

Monday

Monday doesn't like us sad kids, it's the day that it fights us. We don't wanna leave bed, but it finds a way to hold us down and twist us around like a helpless human being in the center of a hurricane.

Eerie Bones

when I starved myself
I felt the sweet burn
of my stomach being empty
and the cold slither of skin
every time I opened
and closed my eyes
when I cried, the tears felt warmer
on my freezing skin
and I could feel my bones touch together as I walked

there was no longer
excessive fat
on my body
instead there was
plain skin
and
madness injected
into my brain

I got this idea
that it's all okay
as long as I'm getting thinner
and when I wasn't
it implied I was doing
something wrong

when I starved myself
I began to slowly die
and linger around
instead of walk
I felt lighter
as I ran
and as my bones transformed
from strong
to eerie
I learned what it was like
to die.

maybe

if someone would have
stuck around
when I starved myself
they would have seen
how I was slowly perishing
and helped me
get back
on my crumbling feet

Untitled 6
(for you)

I miss
how you would get upset when I smoked
and how you would take my cigarette
and tell me that
my lungs and
my voice
were both too beautiful
to be ruined

and I miss
how after that
you would take the cigarette
to your mouth
and smoke it yourself

I miss the day
when you gave me a bottle of vodka
instead of
a bouquet of flowers
to ask me to some
stupid party

and I miss how
I could wake up
with you next to me
and not have to worry
if tomorrow
I would wake up alone
or by your side

truth is
as much as I
tell myself
that it's the memories I miss
it's actually you.
I want you
next to me
again

Family Photos and a lost child

sometimes I don't know where to go
when my only option
is somewhere
where I don't feel
I belong

the photos look better
without me
in them
and nothing seems to
be missing

and I miss
the nights with you
where I felt an actual sense
of belonging

too bad
that the places I feel I belong
are the ones that I don't
and the places I feel I don't belong
are the ones where I do

Tunnels

When I was younger
I was always told
to never be scared
because there would always be
a light
at the end of
the tunnel

And you were the light
that shined through my tunnel

And you were the sun
that lit up the streets

You were the roots
holding the tree

Yet
you weren't able
to understand me

But one thing I forgot;
was that
I was the dark
and you
were the light

and no one
ever told me
the light
at the end
of the tunnel
would be

a train.

Fragile Breaths

I have this thing with missing people and places that have treated me horridly. And once I think about it I realize it's mainly because I believe in no evil; and how everything gets better. And you'd think optimism is always a good thing, but sometimes the glass actually is half empty and not half full. So the next time you look at a situation, or even a human being, think about if it's better to leave for good, or just physically leave. Because sometimes I wish I had left certain people and places when I had the chance, you know. Before I got caught in the twisting hurricane that eventually left me alone. The fact is, when you leave, you leave. everything is gone to you and you don't have to think about it anymore. Kind of like a caged bird that is finally let out to sing in the wild where it belongs. But when you physically leave, everything stays with you. You end up laying alone in bed at night reaching out to someone who is no longer there and calling a dog that is still at his house. You visit all the museums with your friends hoping they'll fill the hole he left you with but nothing is enough and eventually your mind begins to race and your heart beats faster than ever as you realize that instead of the taste of his coffee stained tattooed tobacco lips you are left with blood in your mouth.

Child Of the Universe

I grew up
on the idea
that I am
a child
of the universe
you know,
that I'm
no less
important than
the trees
or the plants
or the sun

and whenever
I was happy
I told myself it's
just the universe
rewarding me
for something
I've done right

and whenever
I was sad
I told myself it's
just the universe
telling me
I did something wrong
and giving me
it's own
kind of timeout

but now
that I'm going through
this torture
I'm questioning
if the universe
loves it's children
as much
as I was told

it does
or if the universe
just needs
to take out
it's anger
sometimes
and instead
of finding
a productive way
to do it
it takes it out
on it's
children.

Speak

for someone who's so known
for writing
I really suck
at talking

I can write down everything
and have it make
perfect sense
but when I try
to speak
my stomach ties knots
and my throat clogs up
and my vocal chords decide
to not work
in that moment
"um"
"I don't know"
are the best explanations
I can give
and that's sad really
because people
who I speak to
think I'm so
unintelligent
"all she says is um"
"all she says is I don't know"

it's just so hard to talk
it's not even mental anymore
it's become a physical problem
where it's hard to move my
mouth enough
to let words out
and I know exactly
what I want to say
and it's sitting there
perfectly in my mind

yet

when I open my lips to speak
nothing comes out
but an "um"
because all my thoughts
are simply trapped
under my tongue
and she refuses
to let them go

Made in the USA
Middletown, DE
11 June 2016